The Greenbrier®

AMERICA'S RESORT

HISTORY BY **Robert S. Conte, Ph.D.**   POETRY BY **Jeff Daniel Marion**

PHOTOGRAPHY BY **Robin Hood**
PULITZER PRIZE-WINNING PHOTOGRAPHER

GRANDIN HOOD
Publishers

Acknowledgements

The publisher wishes to thank the individuals who graciously contributed time and effort to make this book possible. In particular, the greatest measure of gratitude is extended to Jerry Wayne, Vice President of Sales and Marketing, whose original vision and continuing direction for the project brought the book to successful fruition.

Grateful appreciation also goes to Paul C. Ratchford, Greenbrier President and Managing Director, and to former president Ted J. Kleisner for their enthusiastic support of the project.

Particular recognition is given to Robert S. Conte, Ph.D., The Greenbrier's historian. If ever a guest had a secret desire to experience time travel, he only need spend an hour or so on a Bob Conte tour of The Greenbrier grounds. His store of knowledge and congenial manner bring two centuries of events and celebrity guests to life.

Special appreciation is extended to individual Greenbrier associates for their guidance and patient assistance to all requests made during the photography and research phases of production, including Assistant Managers Jamie McKee and Vic Morgan for their willing and timely response to every request for assistance. A special thanks to Rudy Horst, Director of Grounds, for his invaluable forecasts of blooming periods and foliage, and for his willingness to lend technical support as needed. Also, a salute to Matthew Stewart, Director of Engineering for responding to electrical and lighting requirements at unusual hours. Thanks to Lynn Swann for arranging photo subjects and proofing and to Linda Walls for providing the historic White Sulphur Springs bottles seen on page 11, part of her extensive collection of Greenbrier memorabilia. To Robert Harris, Director of Outdoor Sports and Recreation and Hill Herrick, Head Golf Professional is extended our personal thanks for providing guidance and support for photography of the Greenbrier's courses. And to Jim Crews, a special note of gratitude is offered for his assistance with horse activities and a memorable tour of Kate's Mountain.

Finally, no tribute to The Greenbrier is complete without recognizing the warmth of Greeter Frank Mosley, whose nearly half century of gracious service is the epitome of Greenbrier style and tradition.

VIEW FROM THE GOLF ACADEMY ON THE MEADOWS COURSE
PREVIOUS SPREAD: NORTH ENTRANCE FORMAL GARDENS AT DUSK
ENDPAPERS: MURALS FROM THE VIRGINIA ROOM PAINTED BY WILLIAM C. GRAVER IN 1930

THE GREENBRIER: *America's Resort*

Published by:
Grandin Hood Publishers
1101 West Main Street
Franklin, Tennessee 37064
www.grandinhood.com

Designed by Robertson Design, Inc., Brentwood, TN
Proofreading by Lisa Grimenstein, Columbia, TN
Photography lighting by Randy Powers, Nashville, TN
Prepress by iocolor, Seattle, WA
Printed in China through Asia Pacific Offset, Inc.

ISBN: 0-9771281-3-X

Contents

LEFT: STATUE OF HEBE, GODDESS OF YOUTH, ATOP THE SPRINGHOUSE

Introduction

The classic Georgian architecture of the majestic Greenbrier resort and the breathtaking beauty of the Allegheny Mountains provide a striking and remarkable spectacle, no matter the season. This book is a window to that beauty, capturing the unparalleled magnificence of spring, summer, autumn, and winter at The Greenbrier.

With spring, the buds on the trees and colorful tulips create a palette of youthfulness, a time when the earth is being reborn. Just as the robins remind us all that spring is here, so too, does the return of color to our mountain estate.

As the flowers and trees around us blossom into summer, the cool mountain breezes provide a respite and the opportunity to enjoy our surroundings and the variety of activities that abound on our 6500-acre resort.

Perhaps the most remarkable season of all is autumn, when the leaves become vibrant shades of red, yellow, and orange. It is truly spectacular to see the white columns of The Greenbrier surrounded by mountains of vivid colors.

In winter, lush blankets of fresh-fallen snow cover the ground and remind us of quieter times. A horse-drawn sleigh full of friendship and laughter glides across the North Lawn, and families bundle together, creating a special memory.

For more than two centuries, The Greenbrier has witnessed the changing of seasons. Each season, with its own unique beauty, brings a sense of welcome and hospitality, just as we welcome our guests to our home in the mountains. From our humble beginnings as a cottage community, serving as a resting spot for travelers seeking the benefits of our sulphur springs, to today's luxurious resort setting, the world around us has given our guests the gift of nature.

Paul C. Ratchford

President & Managing Director

Left: Entrance Gate

Previous Spread: 18th greens of The Greenbrier Course (left) and The Meadows Course (right)
Following Spread: Rhododendrons and the Front Entrance

OVER THE YEARS, The Greenbrier has come to mean many things to many different people. To some, the name stands for lush golf courses. To others, it represents pampering service. To still others, the name brings to mind fine dining in a memorable setting. But if you talk to someone who has spent any length of time at the resort in White Sulphur Springs, West Virginia, they will invariably get around to mentioning the quiet sense of history that gently pervades the property.

That history goes back almost to the beginning of the United States. In 1778, a local settler found her way to the spring of sulphur water at the center of today's resort and she bathed there to relieve her rheumatism. Traditionally, the founding of The Greenbrier is dated from this event, but the resort actually evolved quite slowly. It is difficult today to imagine the late eighteenth-century isolation of this small upland valley that was due to the lack of transportation. Migrating bison first traversed a route through the gaps and valleys of the daunting mountainous landscape. Shawnee Indians soon followed, then frontier settlers. A stagecoach route was soon developed along the pathway, and after the Civil War, a major railroad came through. Next, early twentieth-century automobile traffic required paving the old stage road, and that highway in turn became the route of today's Interstate 64.

This print from 1845 shows Baltimore Row in the background. Writers often called the resort a "village in the wilderness."

Top: On this 1761 map of Virginia, the site of The Greenbrier is where Howard's Creek (which runs through the golf courses today) branches off from the Green Briar River. The fact that the mountains just to the east are called "The Endless Mountains" gives some idea of how isolated and unknown the region was at the time.

A CHARMING WOOD BLOCK PRINT OF THE PRESIDENT'S COTTAGE, WHICH WAS ORIGI-
NALLY BUILT IN 1835 AS THE SUMMER HOME OF WEALTHY NEW ORLEANS MERCHANT
STEPHEN HENDERSON.

Most of this, however, was many years away for Michael Bowyer, who in 1784
obtained the first deed on the property that eventually developed into today's world-
class resort. Bowyer died in 1808, but he and his family had prepared for the future
by building commercial improvements adjacent to the mineral-water spring, including a dining room and a row of rough but tight log cabins. Ten years later, Bowyer's
son-in-law, James Calwell, inherited the property, and the timing could not have been
better. Calwell was the beneficiary of a much improved transportation system—stage-
coaches could roll right up to his budding resort by the 1820s—the single most important catalyst to the resort's rapid growth.

James Calwell realized that the key to his success was a free-flowing spring of
mineral water with reputed medicinal attributes that steadily attracted thousands
searching for renewed health. Unpleasant-smelling water like his had drawn individuals concerned about their health to ancient spas in Germany, France, Italy, England,

and Eastern Europe for hundreds of years. In this regard, the development of The Greenbrier can best be seen as the process of transporting to the new world the concept and rituals of the famed resort at Bath in England. The medicinal uses of sulphur water could get quite complex, but in its basic outline, one drank the water for internal problems, primarily stomach issues, and one bathed in the water mostly for rheumatism and skin problems. A resident physician was available to guide one through the process. Because the sulphur water left a white deposit on surrounding rocks, the resort was called White Sulphur Springs. Visitors shortened that to the simpler and more familiar name, "The White."

THIS 1832 PAINTING BY JOHN H.B. LATROBE OF BALTIMORE SHOWS THE DINING ROOM AT WHITE SULPHUR SPRINGS, WHICH STOOD ABOUT WHERE TODAY'S CROQUET COURT IS LOCATED IN THE CENTER OF THE RESORT PROPERTY.

THE FINEST DEPICTION OF WHITE SULPHUR SPRINGS AT ITS ZENITH AS A COTTAGE-
ONLY RESORT IN THE EARLY 1850s IS THIS BEAUTIFUL LANDSCAPE PAINTING BY THE
GERMAN ARTIST, EDWARD BEYER. THIS VIEW FROM COPELAND'S HILL INCLUDES
THE SPRINGHOUSE (LEFT) AND THE COTTAGES IN THE BACKGROUND (LEFT TO
RIGHT), ALABAMA ROW, THE PRESIDENT'S COTTAGE, PARADISE AND BALTIMORE

ROWS, AND THE COLONNADE ESTATE HOUSE. THE STRUCTURES IN THE FOREGROUND
HAVE BEEN REPLACED BY SPRING ROW. TODAY'S GREENBRIER HOTEL IS TO THE
RIGHT OF THE IMAGE, AND THE GOLF CLUB, OUTDOOR POOL, AND INDOOR TENNIS
CENTER ARE TO THE LEFT.

One great heyday in the resort's history occurred in the thirty years before the Civil War when powerful, wealthy, and influential members of Southern society trekked, in the summer months, "up to The White to take the waters." James Calwell embarked on a sustained construction campaign in the 1830s to accommodate the swelling demand by creating a series of cottage rows aligned around the White Sulphur Spring—which he grandly demarcated with the classically designed Springhouse that has formed the core of the resort ever since. Soon he completed the earliest buildings on today's property: Alabama, Louisiana, Paradise, and Baltimore Rows. One structure, now known as the President's Cottage Museum, indicates how prestigious The White had become—between 1838 and 1860 five sitting U.S. presidents stayed in that cottage while vacationing and, presumably, doing some politically advantageous meeting and greeting. Together these cottage rows formed what contemporaries called "a neat little village in the wilderness." The porches of these cottages allowed their occupants to take advantage of broad mountain views and, perched at an elevation of 2,000 feet, catch cooling breezes, avoiding the notoriously hot and humid lowland summers.

OF ALL THE PROMINENT POLITICAL FIGURES WHO VISITED WHITE SULPHUR SPRINGS IN THE NINETEENTH CENTURY, THE MOST FREQUENT GUEST WAS "THE GREAT COMPROMISER," HENRY CLAY, OF KENTUCKY. FOR THIRTY YEARS BEFORE THE CIVIL WAR HE WAS THE "UNOFFICIAL HOST" AT THE RESORT, WHERE HIS RHETORICAL AND SOCIAL SKILLS WERE WIDELY ADMIRED.

THE OLDEST KNOWN PHOTOGRAPH (ACTUALLY A DAGUERREOTYPE) OF THE SPRINGHOUSE, TAKEN IN THE 1850S.

EDWARD BEYER'S 1858 PRINT OF WHITE SULPHUR SPRINGS, WITH THE NEWLY BUILT HOTEL THAT WILL EVENTUALLY BECOME KNOWN AS THE OLD WHITE. THE VIEW SHOWS THE RESULTS OF A MAJOR UPGRADE OF THE PROPERTY IN PREVIOUS YEARS, AND THE LAYOUT OF THE GROUNDS WILL REMAIN MUCH THE SAME FOR THE NEXT FIFTY YEARS. IN 1913, THE GREENBRIER HOTEL WILL OPEN TO THE RIGHT OF THIS AREA AND THE GOLF CLUB AND GOLF COURSES ADDED OFF TO THE LEFT.

An 1835 writer for the *Southern Literary Messenger* captured the incongruity of this stylized social life in such an unlikely location: "After rolling along among the mountains and dense forests, the wild and uncultivated scenery is at once exchanged for the neatness and elegance of refined society and the bustle and parade of the fashionable world." For generations, The White and its successor, The Greenbrier, would be revered for a certain proper, genteel lifestyle, and that reputation was clearly established by the 1830s. This is not to say that people weren't having fun, indeed, the large central lawn surrounded by cottages was the daily gathering spot for games, dances, parties, hunting excursions, flirting, and all sorts of joyful summer activities.

So many people were having so much fun up at The White by the mid-1850s that overcrowding became a serious concern. In response, a small group of Richmond-based investors purchased the resort property—by now close to 7,000 acres of land— and began building new cottage rows and adding the first large hotel. This was known as The Grand Central Hotel, but everybody called it, like the resort, "The White." After a number of years, it became known as "The Old White."

GRAND CENTRAL HOTEL.
GREENBRIER, WHITE SULPHUR SPRINGS.   WEST VIRGINIA.

THE WALKWAY CONNECTING THE OLD WHITE HOTEL (LEFT) AND THE BANDSTAND (RIGHT) WAS KNOWN AS "MELODY LANE." THIS CIRCA-1900 VIEW IS FROM BALTIMORE ROW.

ROOM KEYS FROM THE OLD WHITE HOTEL.

RIGHT: THE ORIGINAL CHINA PATTERN USED IN THE GREENBRIER FROM 1913 UNTIL 1942.

A CLASSIC VIEW OF THE GROUNDS AT THE WHITE IN 1883. WITH COTTAGES, THE RESORT COULD ACCOMMODATE ABOUT 1700 OR 1800 GUESTS, MORE THAN THE TWENTIETH-CENTURY RESORT. THIS IMAGE WAS USED AS THE LETTERHEAD ON RESORT STATIONERY.

For the next one hundred years, White Sulphur Springs was one of the great American railroad resorts. Visitors from northern states and western regions started arriving on expanding rail connections, complementing the traditional southern clientele. Even in the last quarter of the nineteenth century, people were attracted by the quiet sense of history that already gently pervaded the property. Charles Dudley Warner described that sentiment in his 1888 novel, *Their Pilgrimage*, reviewing the resort's role over the years:

> The White Sulphur has been for the better part of a century, as everybody knows, the typical Southern resort, the rendezvous of all that was most characteristic in the society of the whole South, the meeting place of its politicians, the haunt of its belles, the arena of gayety, intrigue, and fashion. If tradition is to be believed, here in years gone by were concocted the measures that were subsequently deployed for the government of the country at Washington, here historic matches were made, here beauty had triumphs that were the talk of a generation, here hearts were broken at a ball and mended in Lovers' Walk, and here fortunes were nightly lost and won.

A POSTCARD VIEW
SHOWING THE
FRONT PORCH OF
THE OLD WHITE
HOTEL CIRCA 1908.

THESE YOUNG WOMEN
FROM RICHMOND DISPLAYED THE
HEIGHT OF SUMMER FASHION IN THE LATE 1890S.

ULTIMATELY, The Chesapeake and Ohio Railway transformed The White into The Greenbrier. At the dawn of the twentieth century, the time was at hand for an infusion of new capital as well as a reinvention of The White's resort business, and both were provided by the C&O's 1910 purchase of the property. The railroad acted upon its direct interest in the resort's continued survival—travelers to The White generated important passenger ticket sales. The C&O immediately initiated several major construction projects at the old resort. Within a few years, White Sulphur Springs featured a new year-round hotel, The Greenbrier, a modern Mineral Bath Department to compete with the best in Europe, an enormous indoor swimming pool, tennis courts, a clubhouse, a nine-hole golf course designed by Alexander Findlay, and an eighteen-hole course designed by the reigning American master craftsman of golf architecture, Charles Blair Macdonald.

INSET: Following the custom at European spas, the sulphur water was pumped into The Greenbrier, as shown in this circa-1920 photograph. This spring room was replaced in 1930.

BELOW: The Greenbrier Hotel as it looked when it opened on October 1, 1913. This is the central section of today's hotel; it was substantially enlarged in 1931.

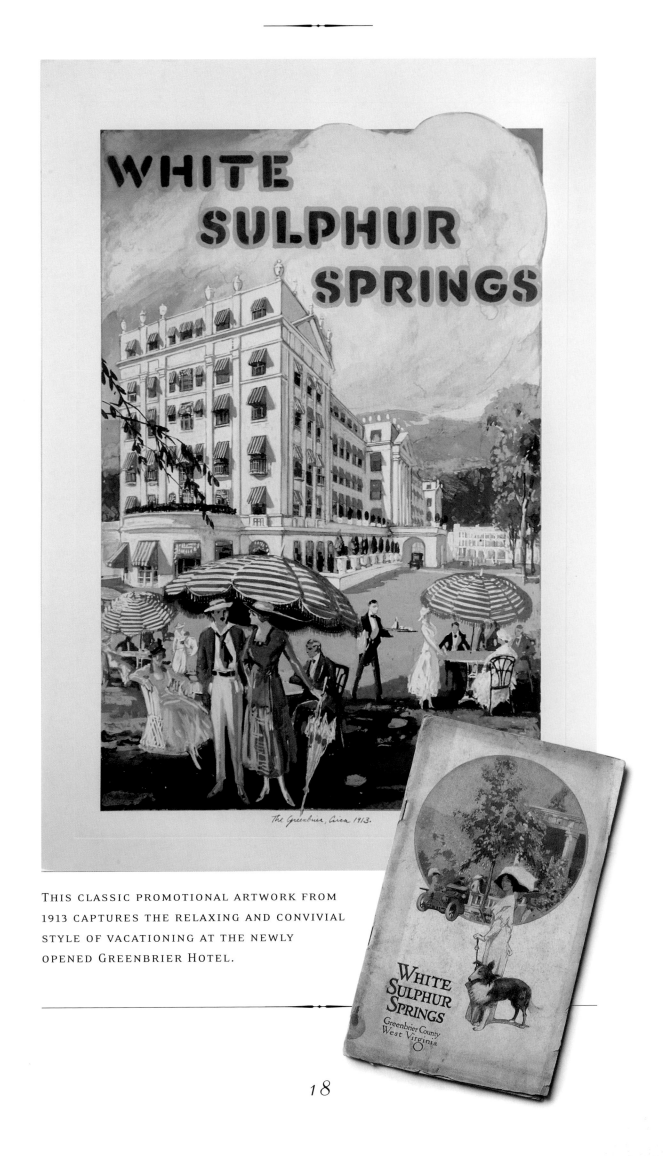

This classic promotional artwork from 1913 captures the relaxing and convivial style of vacationing at the newly opened Greenbrier Hotel.

The Greenbrier Hotel opened on October 1, 1913; the next year was the first full season for a revitalized resort that instantly took its place as one of the finest in North America. In those early years, The Greenbrier promoted itself as "A European Cure in America" to divert those sailing on grand ocean liners for European spas. The Greenbrier was well positioned to take advantage of the Roaring Twenties, which became one more heyday in the resort's history. When the U.S. economy took off in the 1920s, "High Society" and its younger counterpart, the "Smart Set," discovered that The Greenbrier provided a relaxing interlude between busy social seasons in Palm Beach and Newport. The burgeoning media's fascination with celebrities brought extensive coverage in newspapers and magazines. Conde Nast, the publisher of *Vogue* and *Vanity Fair*, was a frequent visitor. Newspapers loved golfing photographs of Bethlehem Steel's Charles Schwab, Mr. "Big Steel" in America. Pictures of Bobby Jones teeing off on The Old White were featured in America's sports pages. Golf at The Greenbrier proved so popular, especially after the 1922 Women's National Championship on Old White, that a second eighteen-hole course opened in 1924, christened The Greenbrier Course.

ABOVE: COMMEMORATIVE SILVERWARE PRODUCED AS PART OF THE ROBERT E. LEE WEEK ACTIVITIES OF THE 1930S.

LEFT: ROBERT E. LEE'S VISITS IN THE 1860S WERE COMMEMORATED IN COSTUME BALLS IN THE 1930S. THIS DANCE, KNOWN AS THE "WHITE SULPHUR RILEY," WAS POPULAR DURING THE YEARS LEE VISITED AND IS REVIVED HERE IN 1938.

This dramatic 1931 photograph shows two steam locomotives pulling up along the main line and siding of the newly built train station. From 1870 to 1970 the vast majority of guests arrived at and departed from The Greenbrier by train.

ABOVE LEFT: This advertisement for the new 1932 Chevrolet truck ($600!) shows a typical scene upon arrival at the train station across from The Greenbrier's front gate.

The Greenbrier Hotel's success made the nineteenth-century Old White Hotel obsolete, and therefore, in 1922, the old summer hotel was demolished. As the prosperous twenties wore on, however, the resort's guest room inventory was insufficient to meet increasing demand. As a result, the C&O Railway developed ambitious plans by 1928 to substantially increase the size of the hotel – it doubled capacity by adding the Virginia Wing to the south (designed with lines meant to echo Mount Vernon) and what is now the signature North Wing facade. Architect Philip Small produced more than a larger building; he imagined a Southern manor house design reflecting the resort's antebellum history. From the exterior, the structure appears much the same today.

ODDLY ENOUGH, A RESORT OWNED BY A RAILROAD WAS ONE OF THE FIRST TO PROVIDE A PRIVATE LANDING STRIP FOR GUESTS.

BELOW: MEETING MR. VANDERBILT'S AIRPLANE IN 1938. THIS LANDING STRIP STOOD WHERE THE SNEAD GOLF COURSE IS LOCATED TODAY.

The Greenbrier Airport   White Sulphur Springs, W. Va.

22

On the golf front, hiring a new assistant pro in 1936 dramatically increased The Greenbrier's national recognition. Sam Snead hadn't seen much of the world at that point, but his profile changed quickly in the upcoming years. In a meteoric two-year rise from an unknown to the PGA tour's leading money winner, Sam made a memorable impact on a golf world lacking a dominant figure since Bobby Jones retired.

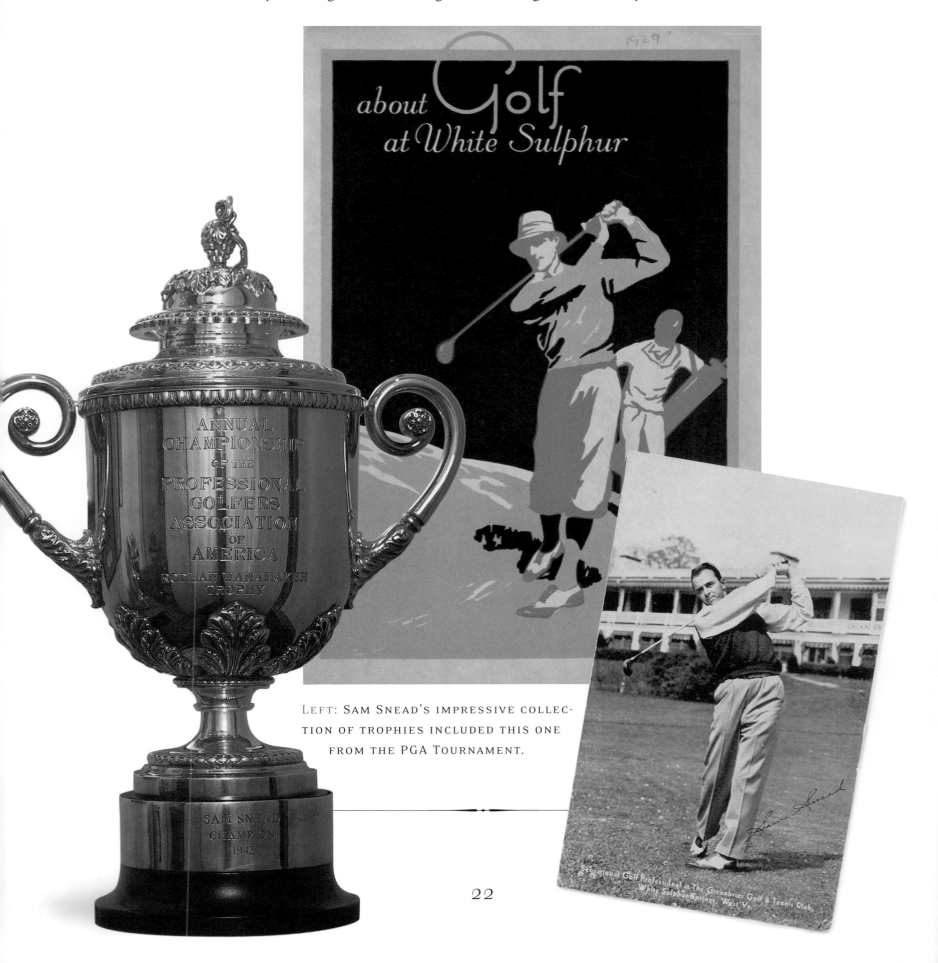

LEFT: SAM SNEAD'S IMPRESSIVE COLLECTION OF TROPHIES INCLUDED THIS ONE FROM THE PGA Tournament.

ABOVE: THE OBSESSION WITH GOLF BEGAN WITH THE OPENING OF ALEXANDER FINDLAY'S NINE-HOLE COURSE IN 1910 AND SHOWS NO SIGN OF LETTING UP.

LEFT: ACTOR DOUGLAS FAIRBANKS OUT ON THE LINKS IN OCTOBER 1934.

RIGHT: NEW YORK YANKEE LOU GEHRIG SHOWS HIS FORM ON THE GOLF TEE IN OCTOBER 1932.

*S*OMETIMES The Greenbrier appears to be a universe unto itself; other times it is absorbed into larger global circumstances. The Second World War was just such a time, when the U.S. government drew The Greenbrier into national service in two distinct ways. First, a few days after the Pearl Harbor attack, State Department officials called The Greenbrier seeking help in facing an urgent problem. Fully-staffed Japanese, German, and Italian embassies operated in Washington, D.C., and, just as important, American embassies functioned overseas in Tokyo, Berlin, and Rome. Geneva conventions required the State Department to exchange hundreds of diplomats, support

personnel, and their families and thus requested that The Greenbrier act as a temporary

housing location while complicated transportation arrangements were negotiated.

Diplomatic parties began arriving on December 19, 1941.

The Greenbrier remained closed for seven months; diplomats and their families

were regarded as regular guests per State Department instructions. Staff size, service,

and meals remained the same even though these particular guests could not step off the

property and U.S. Border Patrol agents secured the resort's perimeter. The Greenbrier

eventually hosted 650 Germans, 400 Japanese, and 250 Italians, as well as smaller

Hungarian and Bulgarian groups. The Red Cross arranged the complex logistics of the

international exchanges, and the last diplomat departed on July 8, 1942.

BELOW: THE JAPANESE DIPLOMATS AND THEIR
FAMILIES GATHERED AT THE NORTH ENTRANCE
FOR THIS STRIKING PHOTOGRAPH IN MAY 1942.

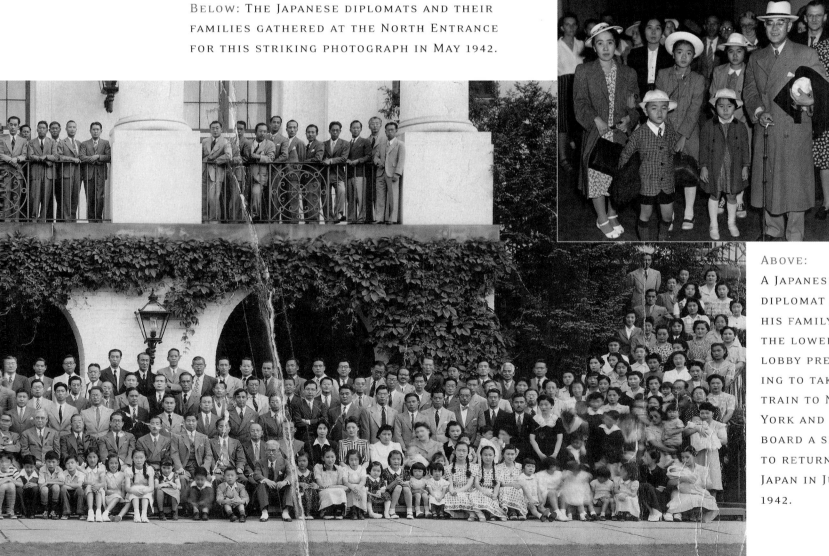

ABOVE:
A JAPANESE
DIPLOMAT AND
HIS FAMILY IN
THE LOWER
LOBBY PREPAR-
ING TO TAKE A
TRAIN TO NEW
YORK AND
BOARD A SHIP
TO RETURN TO
JAPAN IN JUNE
1942.

The C&O now faced a tremendous challenge – bringing the property back to its fabled pre-war luxury level. In a bold step, Robert R. Young decided to rely on the era's most famous and influential interior decorator, Dorothy Draper, and allowed her a designer's dream assignment: create a comprehensive new look throughout the hotel

LEFT: DOROTHY DRAPER WAS KNOWN FOR HER HATS AS WELL AS HER DECORATING SKILLS.

BELOW: DOROTHY DRAPER'S CUSTOM-DESIGNED CHANDELIER IN THE CAMEO BALLROOM BECAME THE SYMBOL OF HER COMPREHENSIVE NEW LOOK FOR THE GREENBRIER'S INTERIOR, AS SHOWN IN THIS 1956 PHOTOGRAPH.

and property using her dramatic imagination and a healthy budget. Nine million dollars and sixteen months later, The Greenbrier reopened with a stunning new interior filled with brilliant colors, enormous black and white marble floors, awesome chandeliers, opulent fabrics, antiques in every alcove, and more floral patterns than anyone could count. A lavish party to celebrate The Greenbrier's re-entry into the world of American high society was held in April 1948. Dorothy Draper received ongoing accolades in the sparkling lobbies, the Duke and Duchess of Windsor attracted magazine photographers' attention, the golf pairing of Bing Crosby and Ben Hogan appeared on newsreels, and Sam Snead returned as the pro and reigned as the man to beat.

ARCHITECTURAL DIGEST MAGAZINE CALLED THE GREENBRIER DOROTHY DRAPER'S "MASTERPIECE." IT WAS THE CULMINATION OF A DISTINCTIVE STYLE SHE HAD BEEN DEVELOPING FOR TWENTY-FIVE YEARS.

When President Eisenhower departed The Greenbrier, he wrote a note to the C&O's president, Walter Tuohy. He thanked Mr. Tuohy for the attentive service and added: "Actually, I am grateful to you for so many things that it is impossible to recount them all, but I want to assure you that I am exceedingly aware of my indebtedness to you and your associates." It is clear in hindsight that the vagueness of that sentence referred to Mr. Tuohy's committing The Greenbrier to a sensitive security project, building an emergency relocation center at the resort for use by the U.S. Congress in case of war. Within weeks, railroad officials and government agents began plotting how to build the bunker and, just as importantly, how to hide it.

Excavation began late in 1958 on Copeland's Hill directly behind the existing hotel. Simultaneously, The Greenbrier announced that a major new addition — the West Virginia Wing — would house The Greenbrier Clinic, offer 85 new guest rooms, and include modern conference facilities. The biggest resort expansion in thirty years created a solid cover story disguising the underground bunker

TOP: BY JANUARY 1960, BUNKER CONSTRUCTION WAS PROCEEDING AT A RAPID PACE ONLY A FEW HUNDRED YARDS FROM THE GREENBRIER HOTEL.

CENTER: THE WEST VEHICULAR TUNNEL WAS BUILT NEAR THE END OF BUNKER CONSTRUCTION. HERE WORKMEN ARE PREPARING TO INSTALL THE TWENTY-FIVE-TON BLAST DOOR.

BOTTOM: LOOKING WEST DURING BUNKER CONSTRUCTION IN JUNE 1959, THE DEEP CUT WAS USED AS A CONSTRUCTION ROAD AND THEN BECAME THE SITE OF THE WEST VEHICULAR TUNNEL ENTRANCE.

construction. The tactic was called "hiding it in plain sight." Indeed, a historic day in American golf history occurred on The Greenbrier Course during bunker construction in May 1959, when Sam Snead scored an astounding 59. Media coverage was extensive, yet no one noticed that not far from the eighteenth green, heavy equipment had virtually completed digging out the bunker's site.

Building the West Virginia Wing was the above-ground project that hid the secret project directly below it. Two buildings were constructed at the same time, one stacked atop the other. To all questions, the response was simple and straightforward: "We are adding a new complex to better serve our guests." With construction complete in 1962, a new Greenbrier-government partnership began — resort staff, mostly engineering employees, worked as needed inside the facility to fulfill a primary goal of keeping the bunker at "a constant state of operational readiness." For the next thirty years The Greenbrier was literally a resort with a secret mission; it led an overt and covert existence. Below ground, a facility remained ready for activation should the most dreaded twentieth-century nightmare come to pass — nuclear war. Above ground, a beautiful, romantic, and lavish resort effortlessly continued providing its bounty to the public.

THIS PHOTOGRAPH BECAME THE BUNKER'S ICONIC IMAGE BECAUSE IT CONVEYS THE OMINOUS COMBINATION OF STEEL AND CONCRETE NECESSARY TO CREATE A PROTECTIVE SHELL AGAINST FALLOUT IN CASE OF NUCLEAR WAR. THIS TWENTY-FIVE-TON BLAST DOOR SWINGS SHUT TO COVER A VEHICULAR TUNNEL ENTRANCE.

The West Virginia Wing was not just a decoy hiding the bunker. The Greenbrier Clinic became a nationally recognized center of diagnostic excellence, an early proponent of preventative medicine. With new conference facilities, The Greenbrier achieved a high level of success, working with trade associations, corporate boards, and company retreats. Business conferences at The Greenbrier played a role as informal CEO summit meetings for America's largest and most powerful industries.

GOLF ARCHITECT LESTER GEORGE AND ROBERT HARRIS, THE GREENBRIER'S DIRECTOR OF SPORTS AND RECREATION, ON THE NEWLY RESTORED OLD WHITE COURSE.

Old White began under the direction of golf architect Lester George. He sought to update the course by incorporating characteristics of the original 1913 designer, Charles Blair Macdonald. The challenging results of a paradoxical exercise in looking backward to go forward were clear to The Greenbrier's new Golf Pro Emeritus Tom Watson when he played a ceremonial first round in May 2006.

Overshadowing these new directions in ambition and scale was the creation of The Greenbrier Sporting Club. Announced in April 2000, the project was the single largest re-conceptualization of the resort property in a century, since the building of The Greenbrier Hotel and a golf course in 1913. The fundamental idea was to utilize the enormous acreage that has been part of the resort's property since the Civil War and develop home sites and private club facilities. Earlier plans for similar development were stymied by bunker-related contractual agreements with the government—you can't sell private property that has a secret government take-over clause. In the fall of 2001, owners of the first homes on Copeland's Hill took possession. Development continued in phases, but the project reached a significant maturation point in May 2004 when the splendid Tom Fazio-designed course, The Snead, opened to members on the same day the magnificent Sporting Club Lodge began operations. A private Sporting Club spa, outdoor swimming pool, tennis facility, exercise barn, and horse stables soon followed. All of this, of course, sits adjacent to the multiple existing facilities of The Greenbrier. Initial sales were brisk and the project was clearly an unqualified success.

With that project launched, attention returned to The Greenbrier. In an unprecedented move, The Greenbrier closed for three months in the first quarter of 2007, in the initial phase of yet another series of renovation projects. Not since the U.S. Army's departure sixty years earlier had the hotel been empty of guests. This time the energy was focused on creating a new restaurant, Hemisphere; a new night spot, 38°30; as well as a complete renovation of guest rooms in the hotel's central section. The current efforts reflect the determination of the resort's owners, the CSX

CARLETON VARNEY, THE PRESIDENT OF DOROTHY DRAPER & COMPANY, HAS PROMOTED, EXPANDED AND UPDATED THE FAMOUS DOROTHY DRAPER LOOK THROUGHOUT HIS LEGENDARY CAREER.

Corporation, to maintain the standards of excellence established by their predecessor company, the Chesapeake and Ohio Railway, at the dawn of the twentieth century.

HOWARD'S CREEK LODGE, CREATED USING THE LOGS OF A ONE HUNDRED AND SIXTY-YEAR OLD BARN FROM THE AREA.

Few American institutions can claim that they have essentially been in the same business for two hundred years. The Greenbrier has throughout centuries of change and adaptation remained true to its founding purpose: to provide the most attentive service possible to its guests here at its humble home in the beautiful Allegheny Mountains.

April Twilight

Long green cape billowing,
the old lamplighter begins
his rounds, touching flame to wick
of dogwood and silverbell,
witch-hobble and wood anemone,
sprigs aglow from creekside to meadow,
Greenbrier ridges and rolling fields.

Forget the ashes sifted from winter's
darkest hearth—gone now is wind's
cold whistle through cabin
and down stone chimney.

Come again are the spring peepers
winding this new clock, singing:

Begin, begin

BELLMAN CARTS, FRONT LOBBY PORCH

LEFT: KWANSAN CHERRY TREE AT FRONT ENTRANCE
PAGES 38 & 39: SAUCER MAGNOLIA BLOOMING AT NORTH ENTRANCE
PAGES 40 & 41: KWANSAN CHERRY BLOSSOMS AT FRONT ENTRANCE
PREVIOUS SPREAD: NORTH ENTRANCE TULIPS AT DUSK

THE OLD WHITE TERRACE GARDEN

RIGHT: THE OLD WHITE TERRACE

VICTORIAN WRITING ROOM (DETAIL)

LEFT: TRELLIS LOBBY
PREVIOUS SPREAD: WEST FACADE OF THE GREENBRIER, FROM COPELAND HILL

EARLY DOGWOOD OUTSIDE SAM SNEAD'S AT THE GOLF CLUB

RIGHT: DON "CHIEF" CRUMP HAS BEEN GREETING GOLFERS AT THE GOLF CLUB FOR OVER FIFTY YEARS

PREVIOUS SPREAD: NORTH ENTRANCE FORMAL GARDENS

GREENBRIER HEAD GOLF PROFESSIONAL HILL HERRICK PROVIDES ADVICE ON GREENBRIER NO. 16.

RIGHT: VIEW ACROSS HOWARD'S CREEK TO THE FAMOUS 1ST HOLE OF THE OLD WHITE COURSE
PREVIOUS SPREAD: 2ND GREEN, THE MEADOWS COURSE

DOORMEN DARNELL HUNTER, SHAWN MAYO, JERRY SEAMS AND DALE MANN REPRESENT OVER 90 YEARS OF GREETING GUESTS TO THE GREENBRIER.

RIGHT: EAST FACADE OUTSIDE PARADISE ALLEY

ENTRANCE TO THE GREENBRIER CLINIC, WEST VIRGINIA WING

PREVIOUS SPREAD: SPRINGHOUSE, FROM ALABAMA ROW

PRESIDENT'S COTTAGE MUSEUM

THE SPRINGHOUSE, FROM SPRING ROW

LEFT: FORMAL GARDENS, FROM THE CARLTON VARNEY SUITE
PREVIOUS SPREAD: NORTH ENTRANCE AT DUSK

PORTICO OF FRONT ENTRANCE

PREVIOUS SPREAD: NORTH ENTRANCE FORMAL GARDENS

TRUMPETER SWANS ON SWAN LAKE

Mid-June at The Spring

This endless afternoon whispers, Come
sip my elixir under sky where clouds
swim in a current deep and blue
as the perfect dream of sleep.

Years and generations have come, seekers
believing the waters a cure, drawn
by mysteries buried in earth.

Here is the hourglass of time, its truth
a quiet and constant trickle, traveling
mile after mile on the long journey

to your hand, your cup: each drop
a moment of Now, Now

MANTEL IN THE LOBBY BAR

RIGHT: THE VICTORIAN WRITING ROOM, FROM THE CAMEO BALLROOM
PAGE 85: THE SPRINGHOUSE
PREVIOUS SPREAD: AMTRAK'S FAMED CARDINAL EASTBOUND TRAIN NAVIGATES THE SCENIC
NEW RIVER GORGE IN ROUTE TO THE GREENBRIER

THE GREENBRIER'S GREENHOUSE

RIGHT: RUDY HORST, DIRECTOR OF GROUNDS
PREVIOUS SPREAD: CAMEO CORRIDOR

97

INDOOR POOL CORRIDOR

LEFT: THERESA AMBLER SERVES EARLY MORNING COFFEE TO GUESTS IN THE MAIN LOBBY
PREVIOUS SPREAD: BELLMAN JAMES POTEAT

October Morning

Fog wraps its cold shawl across ridges
of Kate's Mountain, drapes shoulders
of trees who spring and summer
have whispered, their murmurings
like water over shoals:

so many secrets,
so many secrets

Now they lift their voices, shouting
in bright tones: we are the crayon colors
of memory; yellow for the rising
harvest moon fading soon
to parchment of cornhusks;
crimson and russet for the blood
of ancestors. Tawny, so many leaves
drifting to earth, leaf mound to dust.

Here is the musk of history, pages
turned, leaf smoke of what was,
now rising from earth, fading and gone.

THE SPRINGHOUSE IN AUTUMN

PAGE 101: 7TH HOLE, THE OLD WHITE COURSE
PREVIOUS SPREAD: CARRIAGE RIDE AT THE FRONT ENTRANCE

GABLE DECORATION ABOVE THE WEST TERRACE

CARRIAGE DRIVER FRANKLIN "RICHIE" HUFFMAN AND FRIENDS

RIGHT: EQUESTRIAN DIRECTOR SAMANTHA POSTEN
PREVIOUS SPREAD: SWAN LAKE AND KATE'S MOUNTAIN

TRUMPETER SWANS ON FROZEN SWAN LAKE

PREVIOUS SPREAD: 7TH HOLE, THE OLD WHITE COURSE

CHALYBEATE SPRINGHOUSE ALONG VALLEY VIEW TRAIL

GREENBRIER LESSONS IN FALCONRY, THE HISTORIC "SPORT OF KINGS"

HORSEBACK RIDING, FROM THE NORTH ENTRANCE

Predawn fog at the Front Entrance

Right: The Springhouse at Christmas
Page 119: Snow-covered 18th tee, The Old White Course
Pages 120 & 121: Clearing storm over the North Entrance
Previous Spread: Howard's Creek meanders through The Old White Course

Virginia Wing Gardens

Right: Carriage ride from the North Entrance

GINGERBREAD TOWN, MAIN LOBBY

LEFT: CHRISTMAS TREE, MAIN LOBBY
PREVIOUS SPREAD: CAMEO BALLROOM AT CHRISTMAS

CARRIAGE RIDE TO THE SPRINGHOUSE

RIGHT: CHRISTMAS AT THE GREENBRIER
PAGES 138 & 139: SLEIGH RIDE ON VALLEY VIEW TRAIL
PAGES 140 & 141: GAZEBO AT CHRISTMAS
PREVIOUS SPREAD: CROSSING HOWARD'S CREEK
FOLLOWING SPREAD: EARLY MORNING FOG ON THE FRONT DRIVE